Young Muslim

Contents

1. Iman / Belief

2. Family Structure

3. Duties & Responsibilities

4. Rights

5. Manners / Respect

6. Smart Approach

7. Conclusions

Family Structure

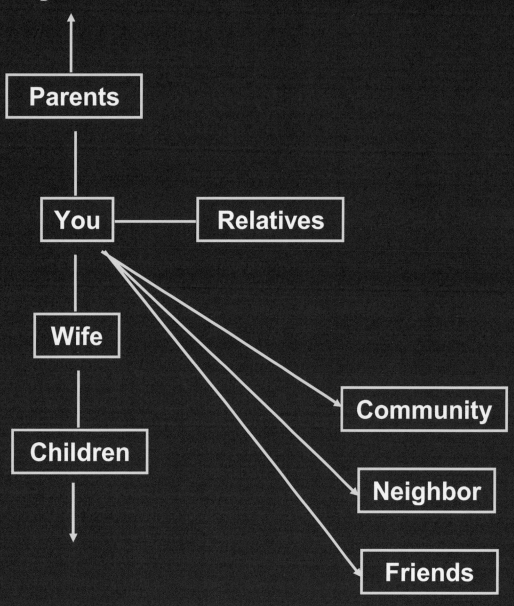

Iman / Belief

- Islam - universal religion for **all mankind**.

- Islam - means submission to the will and law of God.

- Islam - Other meaning is **peace** (through God)

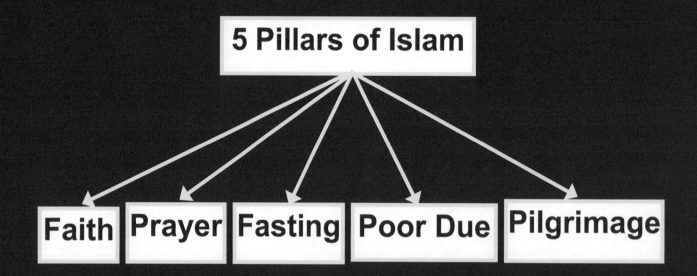

5 Pillars of Islam

Faith | **Prayer** | **Fasting** | **Poor Due** | **Pilgrimage**

Family / Parents - 1

1. And We have enjoined on man to his parents. His mother bore him in weakness and hardship upon weakness and hardship, and his weaning is in two years - give thanks to Me and to your parents. Unto Me is the final destination. *(31:14).*

2. A person asked Rasul ﷺ: Who has the most right to my good company?

    > He answered: **Your mother**.
    > The man asked: And then who? He said: **Your mother**.
    > The man again asked: And then who?
    > He again answered: **Your mother**.

    Then the man asked yet again: And then who? Rasul then said: **Your father**. *(Bukhari, Muslim).*

3. Abdullah bin Mas'ud asked Rasul ﷺ to tell him what deed is most beloved to Allah. Rasul answered: Being dutiful to parents. When asked what next, he said: Jihad in the way of Allah. *(Bukhari, Muslim)*

4. A man came to Rasul ﷺ to seek permission to take part in jihad. Rasul asked him: Are your parents alive? He said: Yes. So Rasul ﷺ told him: Go and strive on their behalf. *(Bukhari, Muslim).*

Parents Etiquette - 1

1. Behave nicely with your parents; in their old age, take care of them no matter how difficult it is, do not even say "oof" to them.

2. A glance at your parent with affection will give you reward of an accepted Hajj.

3. Talk politely, respectfully with them. Do not get upset with them. Whoever takes good care of his parents, Allah will increase his life-span with His blessings. Pray for your parents by saying: *rabbir humhuma kama rabba yane sagira.* (Oh Lord! Have mercy on them the way they used to be merciful to us in our infancy).

4. Always obey them if they do not go against Islam. Be helpful to them by doing housework for them. Help them raise younger siblings. Don't be too demanding beyond their capacity. Show appreciation when they do good things for you. Overlook their faults. Use kind words when you try to correct them.

Parents Etiquette - 2

5. In case one's parents are not Muslim or un-Islamic, you should still care for them, respect them, and obey them unless they order you to disobey Allah; try to encourage them to Islam kindly, gently and with the wisdom of Quran.

6. Do not travel without their permission.

7. Prefer their needs to yours.

8. Your parents' rights over you are: you make sure they do not go hungry and have clothes and a place to live; take care of them in their sickness according to your capacity.

9. In case they are dead, ask for forgiveness for Muslim parents. Try to pay off their debts. Be kind to their loved ones.

10. Grandparents, uncles, and aunts on both mother's and father's sides have similar rights.

11. Do not call them by their names but instead say: O my father, O my mother.

12. Remember that the money you spend on your family earns the most reward from Allah.

13. Never break blood relations. If you do, you will be forbidden to enter Paradise.

14. If you take an oath, which is causing hardship to your family, you must break it and pay recompense for breaking the oath.

15. "Be at your mother's feet and there is the Paradise." *(Ibn Majah, Sunan, Hadith #2771)*

One Way Ticket

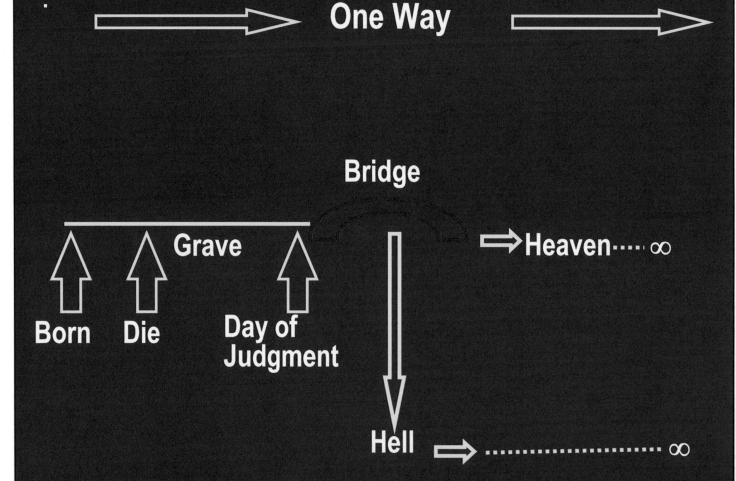

Smart People of the Hereafter

Status in Heaven	=	Good Deeds	-	Sins

Positive Asset **Right Hand** **Heaven**

Negative Asset **Left Hand** **Hell**

Virtues of Da'wah

Allah says…

Shall I tell you ….**business** that will save you from painful punishment?

✓ …you **believe** in Allah and the Messenger (ﷺ)

✓ …**strive**…with **wealth** & **lives**….

- -

✓ Allah will **forgive** your sins,

✓ **Enter** you into paradise…the **great success**.

(As-Saff:10-12)

Why Da'wah is Highly Rewarded?

Da'wah is the <u>Mother</u> of all Deeds.

$$D1 = \sum D11 + \sum D21 + \sum D31 + \ldots \ldots \sum Dn1$$

Best Strategy *for* Hereafter...

- ➤ **Engage**: Maximum Da'wah (*Highest rewards*).

- ➤ **Parallel Processing**: Do many jobs at the same time. People use ~5% brainpower, 95% idle. Do more. **Make your own package**.

- ➤ **Rasul's Activity**: 23 years...so much done. **Unlimited** potential. Room for improvement.

- ➤ **Intentions**: **Plan** on good deeds...in Da'wah, help Muslims, fikr of Rasulullah (ﷺ).

- ➤ **Prepare**: Don't oversleep, overeat or be a couch potato. Companions used to raise horses for struggle.

How To Play it Safe...

✓ **Repent**: Rasul (ﷺ) used to repent 100 times / day

(*Muslim*)

✓ **Get out of Haram**: **Don't gamble & be a loser**.

✓ **People at Border**: **Good Deeds ~ Sins**.

Add Nafl salat, read Quran, give Sadaqa,

go for Da'wah, help Muslims. **Do extra**.

✓ **Protect** Hereafter *constantly*.

Saitan works 24 hrs to destroy assets by

silently luring people into major sins.

Either you **Build or Destroy** assets at any time.

A Momen is always careful & vigilant.

Sins Converted into Good Deeds *(Best Deal...)*

...Repent, Believe...do Good deeds, Allah...exchange... sins with good deeds. (*Al-Furqan:70*)

Do it **NOW...**

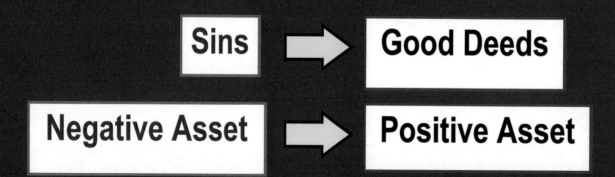

Prophet ﷺ says...

Rasul ﷺ said: You should do 5 things before 5 conditions happen...

1. Use your **Time** properly when you are <u>free</u> before you become **busy.**

2. Use your **Money** for <u>good cause</u> before you **ran out**.

3. Use your **Youth Life** <u>before</u> you become **old**.

4. Use your **Good Health** for <u>good cause</u> before you become **sick**.

5. Use your **Life** for <u>good deeds</u> before you **die**.

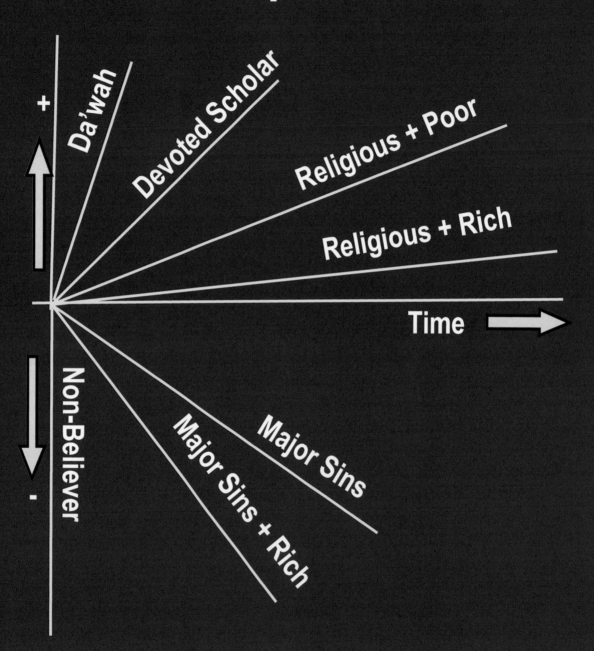

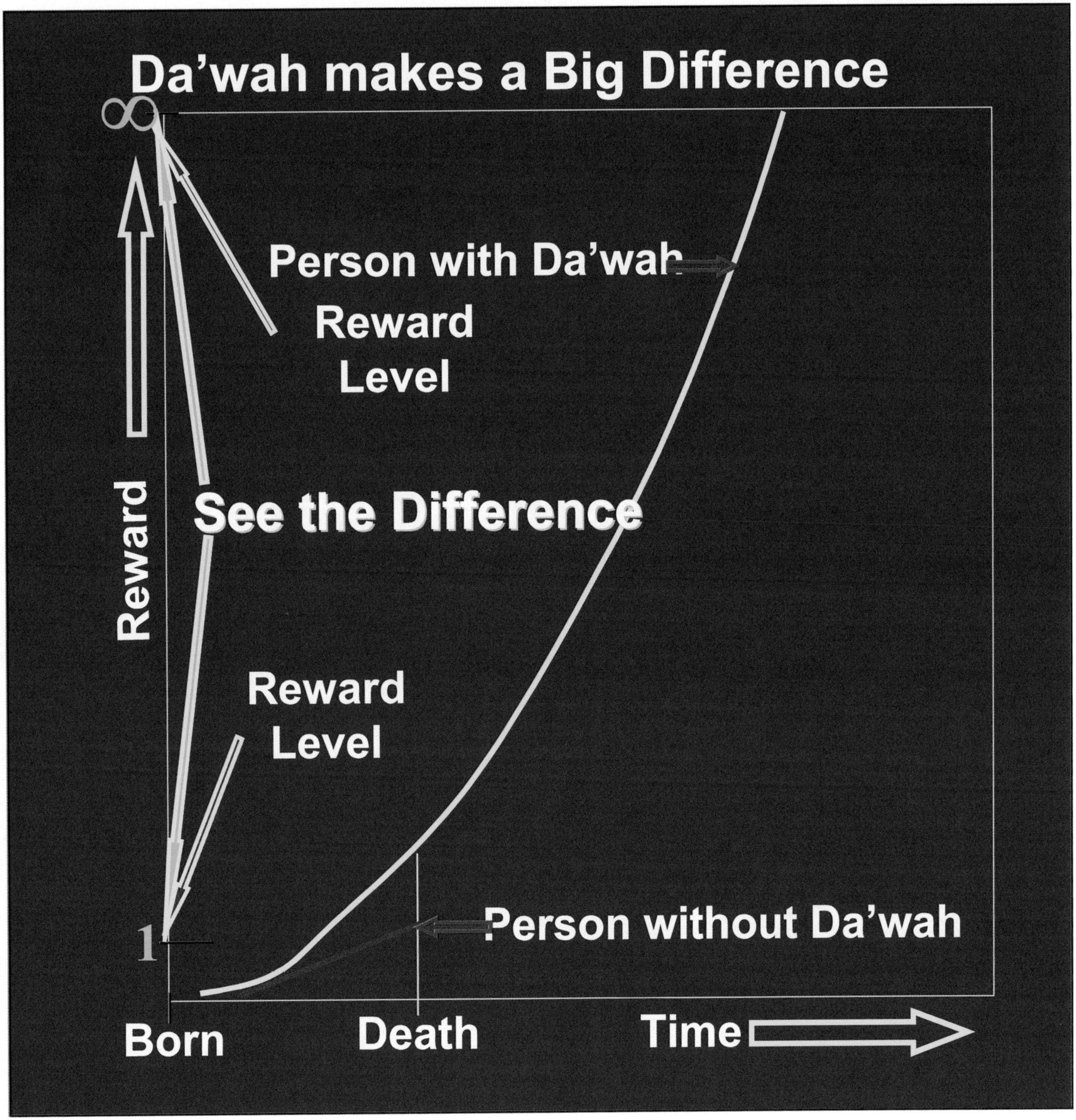

Da'wah makes a Big Difference
∞
Person with Da'wah
Reward
Level
Reward
See the Difference
Reward
Level
1
Person without Da'wah
Born
Death
Time

Roadmap to Heaven...

1. **Don't violate** rights.

2. **Produce highly paid** good deeds.

3. **Excessive personal** good deeds.

4. **Make life-style** very <u>simple</u>, <u>low profile</u>.

5. **Be prepared to leave the world at any time**.

Goals for the Smart People

Goal of Super Smart:

1. Highest Possible reward: **Jannatul Ferdous**

2. Neighbor of Rasul (ﷺ)

Prophet's Neighbor in Heaven...

You can visit, invite, talk with him....forever

One who...

- ➤ Brings up an **orphan**

- ➤ **Loves** the Prophet with lots of Salam

- ➤ **Engages** in Islamic Activities, Da'wah

Manners / Behavior

There will be nothing <u>heavier</u> on scale than

<u>good manners.</u> *(Abu Dawud)*

NASA's Vision...

- Failure is not an Option

- If you can dream, we can make it happen

For more information:

Abdul Hye, PhD

281- 488 - 3191

a6h@yahoo.com

www.FinalRevelation.net

Printed in Great Britain
by Amazon.co.uk, Ltd.,
Marston Gate.